INTRODUCTION

H ave you ever wanted to organize a public event? Do you dream of hosting a battle of the bands, concerts, poetry readings, art shows, teach-ins, lectures, and panels? Maybe you already have experience doing this work but you have noticed that inequities from the society-at-large are replicated at your events, despite best intentions.

The goal of this handbook is to provide event organizers of all levels with the tools to make their events accessible, sustainable, and exemplify social justice principles. Whether you are new to organizing or highly experienced, this zine will provide frameworks and practical tips to create inclusive events. Drawing on my experience organizing hundreds of public events, this handbook is useful for small and large events alike.

I0112442

PART I: DEFINING TERMS

Accessibility and Design Justice

When we talk about accessibility, what do we mean? Do we mean that the event is wheelchair friendly? Do we mean that there is a sign language interpreter? Is there a translator for people who do not speak the primary language used at the event? Is there a lactation room for parents? Is there an all-gender bathroom? What about the cost of tickets?

Design justice* is a framework that aims to center the voices of people who are normally marginalized and directly impacted by the outcomes of the design process (including event organizing). Prioritizing accessibility from a design justice perspective, not only benefits individuals with visible or known physical, psychological, or cognitive disabilities, but works to ensure that participants with obvious or non-obvious disabilities and/or chronic health conditions, people of all ages and body types, individuals across the gender spectrum and of all sexual orientations, from all class, racial, and ethnic backgrounds are able to fully engage in the program. Rather than focus on making "accommodations," which creates a burden for the individual participant and acts as a retroactive patch to overcome barriers in an environment or system, accessibility from a design justice standpoint means that you will design your event to be inclusive from the start. The goal is that the event will not require adaptation or modification to remove barriers to participate.

What does this mean for you as an event organizer? This handbook will help you consider accessibility throughout the entire process of planning and hosting an event. These principles will also guide how you promote and disseminate information about and from your event.

*Check out the awesome work by the Design Justice Network! More in the Further Resources section!

MICROCOSM · PUBLISHING

Microcosm Publishing is Portland's most diversified publishing house and distributor with a focus on the colorful, authentic, and empowering. Our books and zines have put your power in your hands since 1996, equipping readers to make positive changes in your life and in the world around you. Microcosm emphasizes skill-building, showing hidden histories, and fostering creativity through challenging conventional publishing wisdom. What was once a distro and record label was started by Joe Biel in his bedroom and has become among the oldest independent publishing houses in Portland, OR. In a world that has inched to the right for 80 years, we are carving out a place in the center with DIY skills, food, bicycling, gender, self-care, and social justice. / Microcosm.Pub

TABLE OF CONTENTS

Feminism and Social Justice

There are many kinds of feminism, including but not limited to Marxist, Socialist, Liberal, Radical, Anarchist, Eco, Decolonial, Indigenous, and Black Feminisms. There are debates and disagreements between feminists involved in these separate groups and within the groups themselves. These labels, furthermore, do not encompass all approaches to feminism. Each form of feminism has offered and continues to bring different strategies to tackle social injustice. I am not interested in imposing a single prescriptive definition of feminism when discussing inclusive event organizing. For me, feminism in the broadest sense is about the social, political, and economic equity of all sexes and genders. Feminism, as defined in this handbook, seeks to create a socially just world and combat the forces of sexism, heterosexism, transphobia, racism, classism, ableism, and colonialism. Feminist and anti-racist writing, activism, research, and art practices deeply influence my approach and exposure to social justice and disability rights movements. Social justice, feminist, and disability rights activism can interweave and inform the ways we approach creating inclusive events.

Sustainability

Sustainability is key to accessible event organizing in two senses: environmental activism and as part of an ethic of care.

Environmentalism and sustainability must be part of our discussion around inclusive organizing as pollution, climate change, and ecological degradation disproportionately affect the most marginalized members of our communities. Waste and dump sites are zoned near communities of color. Toxic oil refineries are placed next to or on Indigenous lands. We must combat environmental racism. Our events cannot be truly inclusive if they contribute to ecological degradation. This handbook will help you consider the environmental impact of your event.

Sustainability, as a framework, also addresses the ability for something to be maintained at a certain rate or level. Here I would like us to consider an ethics of care in which the material conditions of the organizer, presenter/performer, and audience/participant/attendee are taken into account. Organizing events can be laborious and exhausting. Can you organize events in a manner that is sustainable to your wellbeing and health as the host? How can you make sure that the needs of the performers or presenters are met? What is the role of compensation? By placing care and social justice at the center of your organizing work, your events can bolster connection to others and community building. This handbook will help you consider the ways in which your event sustains you and your participants.

PART II: INITIAL PLANNING

Brainstorming: what kind of event

First things first, what kind of event are you organizing? A concert? A rally? A poetry reading? A teach-in? A lecture? A panel? A fire-side chat? Discussion roundtables? An art show? A live taping? A book reading? A coffeehouse open mic? A workshop? A performance?

There are so many forms public events can take. It can be helpful to draw or write out your ideas of how you envision your event happening. In doing so, you can get a sense of what kind of equipment and resources you will require. This process can also help you figure out a schedule.

In your initial brainstorming, it is useful to think about the 5 W and H questions:

Who: Who is your intended audience? Who is your presenter/ performer/entertainment? Is it part of the organizing group (or is it just you)? How many people do you want to/expect to come?

What: What type of event is this? What do you want to happen? What kind of format will the event follow? What amenities will you provide at the event? What kind of equipment will you need? What materials are necessary?

When: What date will the event take place? Is it one day? Is it recurring? Is it part of a series? What time of day will it take place?

Where: Where is the event going to take place? Will it take place in cyberspace? Will you have to rent a venue? Is the venue accessible only by stairs? How much do you have to pay to use the space?

Why: Why are you hosting this event? Why is an event like this necessary? Knowing your intentions and goals beforehand can help you make decisions throughout the planning process.

How: How will you fund the event? How will you advertise? How will you ensure that your event aligns with your values?

The answers to these questions can have a large impact on the inclusivity of your event.

PART III: IN-PERSON EVENTS

You will need to decide whether your event will happen in person, in cyberspace, or in a combination of the two. The choice of in-person vs digital/virtual events influences your ability to reach different communities and audiences. While a digital event means that someone across the planet can participate, not everyone has computers, phones, or access to the internet (or a strong and stable wifi connection). If you hope to congregate folks from your local community, it is likely that you will choose to hold an in-person event. Consider disseminating aspects of the event so that individuals who couldn't attend otherwise can still be involved.

Starting with Space

When it comes to booking spaces or venues for your event, there are a lot of things to consider if you want your event to be inclusive. Cost of renting or using a space can impact whether or not you charge for the event and this in turn can impact who can attend. The availability of the space may affect the date/timing of the event. The structure of the space can also impact accessibility, and the kinds of programming you can offer.

Below are suggestions to consider when choosing a space for your event.

- Can the room only be entered by climbing stairs or a steep hill? Stairs mean that people with reduced mobility and wheelchair users will not be able to attend. If there are elevators, are they wide enough for wheelchairs and scooters?

- Are the door frames of the venue wide enough for a wheelchair or scooter to pass through? 32 inches or 82 cm (preferably wider)? Is there a bump over the threshold? Even a 1 inch or 2.5 cm bump can pose an issue for wheelchair users. Threshold ramps can mitigate this problem.

• Have you allocated space for service animals? Is there access to the outdoors for service dogs?

• If doors are closed, do the doors have lever handles and/or are equipped with an automatic opener? If not, will you have someone at the entrance to welcome people into the room?

• Is there a public transit option for people to travel to the event? Public transport is a class and environmental issue. (If you're in a major metropolitan area, Google has recently added wheelchair accessible routes to Google Maps on both desktop and mobile.)

• Are there designated parking spots near the entrance for people with disabilities?

• Is there a barrier-free path for people to travel from the parking lot or drop-off area to the venue entrance?

• If you are hosting the event in a place with snow or ice, will the paths be cleared?

• If the event is being held at an outdoor site, will the surface be accessible for persons using wheelchairs and scooters?

• If the main entrance is not accessible, is there a sign clearly visible at the front of the building that indicates the location of an accessible entrance? Make sure to circulate information about this information in advance of the event as well.

• Is there a wheelchair accessible washroom/bathroom? Are the sinks reachable from a wheelchair?

• Is there an All-Gender Washroom/Bathroom? If the venue does not have a single use washroom or all gender washrooms, are you able to temporarily change the bathroom signs for the event? The ability to access a washroom is a basic human right. A lack of all gender washrooms can make your event non-inclusive for trans and gender non-binary individuals.

• Is there a space for parents who are nursing? Is there an electrical outlet for breast pumps?

• Will you be able to provide chairs for people who may need to sit? This can be particularly important for, but not limited to, people with various disabilities, the elderly, and pregnant individuals.

• Can you rearrange chairs/ move chairs so that wheelchair users can have a seat at the table? Near the stage? Is it possible to arrange sitting in circles, so that people hard of hearing can see people's faces?

• Will your event take place in one room? Or multiple?

• How will you ensure people with a low-stimuli threshold will be able to find a quieter space?

• Are you able to control the lighting? Fluorescent lighting can cause headaches, which make it difficult to participate.

• Can you guarantee a scent free environment, including in the washrooms? Due to scent sensitivities, which can cause nausea and headaches, ask participants in advance to refrain from using strong perfumes and soaps.

Booking Rooms/Spaces/Venues/Locations

Your budget will also influence your choice of room or venue.

When renting a room, it is important to check:

- the cost per hour (and to account for set up and take down times)

- What equipment is provided and what you have to provide (chairs, tables, sound equipment, etc.)

- Are there limitations regarding what you can do in the space? If you provide food, do you have to use their in-house caterer? How much noise are you allowed to make? Do you have to hire security?

- Are you responsible for cleaning the space? The bathrooms?

- If you are in an outdoor space, do you need a permit?

Free or Low Cost Options

Using free or low-cost spaces is my preference as it means that the event budget (which sometimes is zero dollars) isn't eaten up by the room rental. Depending on the community you are trying to reach, these options may encourage or dissuade participation. Not everyone feels comfortable going to a college campus or an event in a church basement, even though these may be low cost options.

Libraries

Libraries offer more than books (though books are wonderful)! Your local library may have a room for gatherings, may have maker-spaces, and more! Check out what kinds of resources are available. Even if the library isn't the right venue for your event, you might be able to borrow audio visual equipment or other necessary materials there.

Independent Bookstores
Your local independent bookstore can be a great place to hold readings, panels, and lectures. Many offer their spaces for free or low cost.

University or College Campuses/Schools
If you are a student, it is usually possible to rent spaces on campus for free or low cost (especially if you are part of a student group, club, or organization). If you aren't a student, can you collaborate with a student or faculty member for your event to get access to this free space? From classrooms to concert halls, universities and colleges offer a wide variety of spaces.

After graduating high school, I never held an event in a high school again, but that might be an option for you too.

Community Centers
"Community center" is a broad term that can refer to a wide range of resources and spaces available. They are typically public or semi-public locations where members of a community tend to gather for group activities, social support, public information, and other more. They may sometimes be open for use by the whole community or only for a specialized group within the greater community.

Religious Organizations
Some religious groups will rent out their spaces, particularly basements, even to non-community members. These spaces tend to be available at low or no cost. The choice to meet in the basement of a church, temple, or synagogue may deter participation from potential attendees, and potentially create obstacles to accessibility.

Public Parks

While public parks may have rules about the size of the gathering, time of day, and/or require permits, many public parks have bathrooms, running water, and some kind of structure. Using these facilities can be free or low cost.

Local Music and Arts Venues

Depending on the venue, there can be a wide range of fees. Your city or town might have a cafe, restaurant, pub, bar, or gallery that offers free or low cost space or has sliding scales for events. Businesses that are explicit about their feminist, social justice, or anarchist politics tend to have more affordable options.

Your Own Home or Backyard

For a smaller public event, it might be possible to organize an event in your living space. You will need to check with the people you live with if they are comfortable with this decision. Be respectful of your neighbors, especially regarding noise levels. If your aim is an inclusive public event, people may not feel comfortable entering a private residence and it is probably less likely that your home will be accessible for people with mobility disabilities.

It can be helpful to talk to other event organizers from your town to get local tips and tricks. Also if you are going to pay to use a space, it is great if your dollars can support a business or organization that you respect.

Money

Is it possible to organize an event for zero dollars? Yes. However, it is likely that money will be involved in event organizing even if that is in the form of donations. Your decisions around who gets paid, what you pay for, and whether or not you charge for tickets influence the inclusivity of the event.

Speakers and Performers

If your event involves artists, musicians, performers, speakers, or presenters, it is important to recognize that not paying for art and work is a class issue. Only people with financial flexibility and class privilege will be able to routinely work without pay and this limits the kind of art, performance, and ideas that are displayed. As class in the United States and Canada is racialized and gendered, the voices, perspectives, and art by people of color, Indigenous people, women, non-binary, and trans individuals are less likely to be showcased.

This is not to say that people will not volunteer their time and efforts to showcase their work, but if you are paying the venue, vendors, and are also making money as the organizer, it is important that the artists, performers, and/or speakers are paid. Exposure does not pay the rent.

Whenever I contact potential lecturers, panelists, or performers, in the initial email, I always mention compensation. As an organizer, you may have a limited budget. It is important to be honest and forthcoming about what you can pay the people that you are contacting. This way they can decide if the amount is acceptable to them. It is also important to think critically about the amounts you are offering various performers. Women, Indigenous people, and folks of color continue to be paid at lower rates for their work. Be transparent with how you are paying folks.

In addition, there is a difference between financial compensation and honorarium gifts. It is common practice to provide honorarium gifts to Indigenous Elders or knowledge keepers as a sign of reciprocity and respect. These gifts should be culturally appropriate.

Sample initial email (with details for performers from out of town):

Dear ____,

My name is ___ (mention organizational affiliation here, if it pertains). I am the organizer of the _____(event), which is (1-2 sentences of background information about the event) taking place on (time and date— if this is flexible, mention potential dates but state that they are flexible) at (place). I was wondering if you were interested in __(the type of performance, talk, exhibit, etc). We would be able to offer you _____(amount of money) and cover your travel, including hotel stay and a per diem (consider if a speaker or performer is coming from out of town how you will pay for their plane/train/gas, a hotel (or place to stay), transportation, and a potential per diem).

(you can add a sentence here about the date that you would like for them to reply to you)

Thank you for your time and consideration,

(your name)

I like to keep this initial email quite short. In further emails, it is useful to ask the speaker about the kinds of audio visual equipment that you or they may require, if they are comfortable with you filming, photographing, recording, live-streaming, or broadcasting the event. You may request slides or a speech prior to the event in order to provide large print access copies. If you don't know them, you can also ask the speaker preferred pronouns.

The speaker/artist/presenter may also choose to negotiate the pay. It is okay if you are not able to pay them more to say "no thank you." I find being upfront and honest about the budget leads to productive and cooperative discussions.

Paying people promptly is important. Oftentimes people are asked to front the money for their own work and have to wait months to be reimbursed. If you can book the travel for them or have a check or form of payment for performers the day of the event, that is best practice (though depending on your funding, not always possible).

On occasion, performers/speakers may prefer to donate money on their behalf to a cause of their choosing. You can make this option available to them.

Funding

You might be asking, how am I supposed to pay for all of this? What if you have to rent a venue, rent audio visual equipment, and pay performers?

I usually begin planning by imagining I have no budget at all and see what is possible with zero dollars. Then I work from there.

Tickets are one route of funding an event. Selling tickets in advance can help you have a better sense of your budget. There are numerous online portals that can facilitate this process. However, many take a cut of the sale. Read the fine print. Selling tickets at the door is a low-tech way to handle sales, but not everyone carries cash.

Tickets can also create barriers to access. One solution is Pay What You Can (PWYC) or "Nobody Turned Away for Lack of Funds." Sliding scales can be useful or consider tiered ticket prices, such as "students and elders pay a lower ticket price."

If your event is a fundraiser, it can be possible to receive donations. Donated space. Donated performances. Volunteer workers. Fundraisers usually still have some form of ticket or collection of a resource (money, cans, and/or labor (such as people coming together to clean the beach or translate documents for community members)). When asking for donations, I recommend using a similar email template to the one above. However, rather than asking for a person or group to perform, you ask for what you need in a respectful tone.

Sponsors can be another option. As an event organizer, you need to decide if you are comfortable taking sponsorships. Likely this will entail that you advertise for the company, which might feel inappropriate depending on your event. Remember that you are in control of what kinds of companies and organizations you take money from. Maybe there is a local business that reflects your values and would sponsor your event? These partnerships can put your audience in connection with local businesses or channel corporate money towards a cause you believe in.

Universities and colleges can be a great source of funding for events. Even if you are not a student, is it possible to work with a local student group? They often are able to get student activities funding that can pay for speakers, artists, musicians, and performers.

Municipal funding is another great option. It is likely that your town or city has some form of funding available for local events programming. Does your event idea relate to any local community initiatives? Is there a festival, theme, or goal of your municipal government? State, provincial, territorial, and regional funding is a similar option. Many states and provinces offer grants. Consider potential limitations to receiving this type of funding, and how state and municipal control can limit the message or effectiveness of your event.

National and international grants can be more complex, but depending on your project, can be another option. It is important to note that these kinds of grant applications can require hundreds of pages of paperwork and might not be worth completing for many events. I recommend diving into this kind of grant work after you are a more seasoned event organizer.

Foundation and private grants can vary in the kinds of application materials that they require. Money may be available for the kind of work that you are trying to do. Again, I would suggest applying to these kinds of grants after you are already comfortable organizing events as the applications ask about past experience.

Most grants require some form of matching funding. Check if the grant accepts in-kind matching funding. For example, if you plan to hold your event in donated space, with donated sound equipment, and document the show with donated camera equipment, all of that counts as in-kind funding.

A bit of money grows. Funding agencies are more likely to give money and support if they see that you have already gotten some form of funding and support. For my most successful grant application for a speaker and workshop series, which resulted in a $23,455 grant which required 50% matching funding, I began by getting small contributions of 100 dollars. I could then leverage this funding into contributions of 200 and then 500 dollars and then larger contributions. This process is time intensive and required me to write smaller grants to count towards the matching funding. I dedicated 3 months of my life to this work on top of my primary employment. Start small and you can build on this experience.

Workers and Volunteers

Who is working the event? Yes, you and maybe a group of others are the organizer or organizing committee. However, it is likely that the day or night of the event there will be a variety of tasks. It is difficult to be on stage introducing the bands, while sorting out the issue of the missing extension cord, while taking the pictures, and collecting tickets at the door. I recommend, even for a small event, having a dedicated group of folks willing to help with certain tasks. Depending on the scale of the event and the budget, if you are getting paid, pay people doing work at the event if their contribution is significant.

Demographics

Target audience

Who is your target audience? Knowing your target audience can help you determine the date and time to hold the event. This decision will also be influenced by the availability of the venue, but will also help you decide on the venue. Be mindful about who you might be excluding in your mind when you consider the target audience and not default to able-bodied individuals. The point of creating *inclusive* events is to be inclusive.

Date and Time

Timing of the event greatly influences how inclusive your event will be. Your target audience will be key in making this decision. If it is midday, people might not be able to leave their 9-5 office job to attend. If it is after work hours, parents or people who care for elderly family members might not be able to attend. Facilities might not be free or available on weekends. Friday nights can prevent observant Jewish attendees from coming and Sunday mornings could prevent various Christian attendees. There will never be a perfect time for the event, but think about the group you are hoping to target. I try to schedule events of the speaker series that I am doing at a variety of times so that even if the one event is not an option for someone, hopefully at least one time will work.

Childcare

Depending on the time of the event, it may become necessary to provide childcare as an option in order to make the event accessible to parents. See if your town or city has an organization that subsidizes childcare. You can ask people to RSVP in advance if they require childcare and pool together money to make childcare possible at the event itself.

Language, Interpretation, and Captioning

Interpreters work with spoken (or signed) words, conveying a message from one language to another (including sign languages). Translation deals with written texts. Your event may require interpreters and translators.

I live in Montreal, Canada. Quebec is a francophone province and many of our events are bilingual (French and English). I grew up in Southern California where many events included English and Spanish programming. Even when the event has materials and presentations in the most commonly spoken languages, speakers from other language groups can be left out. Deaf and hard of hearing participants may require an interpreter. The location of your event and your target audience will determine your interpretation and translation needs. Make sure that sign language interpreters on a stage are well lit so that audience members are able to see them.

There are international, national, and more local resources for finding interpreters and translators. Internationally, the International Association of Conference Interpreters provides a great tool to find certified professionals: aiic.net. In Canada, the Canadian Translators, Terminologists and Interpreters Council provides a database for certified professionals outside of Quebec cttic.org/chercher.asp.

Within Quebec, see: ottiaq.org/. If you are looking for a translator in the United States, you can also use the American Translators Association, atanet.org.

While auto-captioning tools do not replace real-time interpretation, these tools can assist in making events more accessible. Powerpoint and Google slides offer auto-transcription tools. Microsoft offers an automated translation plug-in which functions as an auto-captioning device when translating from the presenter's language to the same language, such as English to English. This tool also provides a short url where participants can select their preferred language to follow along on their own devices.

Gear and Audio Visual (AV) Equipment

It is likely that your event will require some kind of electronic equipment. If people are speaking, microphones can improve sound quality and projections. People giving a presentation might want a screen to project a powerpoint. Maybe you will show a film. Perhaps a band or DJ will play. You may choose to film or record or livestream the event so that people who cannot attend can still access the event. Decisions surrounding AV equipment can either radically expand or decrease accessibility.

Using AV Equipment to Increase Accessibility

If there is a projection, such as a Powerpoint or Prezi presentation, does the font contrast with the background? Is the font large and clear to read?

Encourage presenters to orally describe what is on the slides. This technique is beneficial for participants that have reduced vision or are blind. It is also a useful practice if the event is being audio recorded.

Consider asking speakers to submit materials in advance so that they can be forwarded to individuals who may not be able to view screens. Along this, making printed copies available (in larger font) can be beneficial to participants.

When playing videos, turn on closed captioning.

Ask presenters to use microphones and have the audience ask questions into a microphone or ask the presenter to repeat the question into the microphone. Speaking loudly is not the same.

Acoustics are important for those with hearing impairment. Limit unnecessary background noise.

Avoid using flashing or overly bright lights, as this can cause sensory overwhelm.

Check if the facility has a hearing loop (sometimes called an audio induction loop). This is a special type of sound system for use by people who use hearing aids. The hearing loop provides a magnetic, wireless signal that is picked up by the hearing aid.

How to Acquire or Rent AV Equipment

First check out what the venue already provides for free. The venue may also offer rentals, which may or may not be the best deal but can potentially save time, hassle, and stress.

If you are affiliated with a university, even if the event is not at a university, you usually have access to an AV room for free or inexpensive rentals. This equipment can range from microphones, video cameras, cameras, and more!

Check out your local library for resources. Again, libraries have more than books! Many have lending libraries with different kinds of equipment.

Borrow from friends.

If none of the above options work or if you need a particular piece of gear, private rental companies exist.

Make sure that you have the batteries or power cords that you need for this equipment with you ahead of the event.

Food and Drink

Does your event involve food? Choices over food and drink can impact the accessibility of your event.

Food

Will you be charging for the food? Cost of food can impact accessibility for participation and is a class issue. However, cheap food usually means that the farm workers, the people working in the food processing plants, the people cooking the food, and/or the people selling the food are not paid a living wage. This is a labor issue. This is also a feminist issue as women disproportionately do the kind of underpaid or unpaid work of preparing food. Furthermore this labor is highly racialized and classed and is intertwined with immigration policies that criminalize workers. Cheap food comes at environmental costs under industrialized food systems that disregard biodiversity, use pesticides, and leads to the destruction of ecosystems. It is a difficult balance to make sure that food is priced so that every worker is properly compensated and that all participants can afford the food. There is rampant cruelty, exploitation, and injustice throughout the food chain, even when serving vegan food. Mixing the price of items available can be one way to address these issues.

When serving food, there are dietary considerations such as vegan, vegetarian, kosher, and halal, as well as common allergens such as nuts, gluten, and soy. If the event involves a caterer, I try to order food that will meet as many dietary considerations as possible at once. Tasty vegan food with a gluten free option tends to accommodate most participants. However, food carries cultural significance. Depending on your event's objectives, you may make different choices surrounding food.

Drink

Will you be serving alcohol? This may limit the age of participants for the event. It can also impact who might feel welcome to attend the event. People who wish to stay sober may refrain from attending.

The choice to serve alcohol may also require a permit. Check far in advance, as liquor permits can be difficult to obtain depending on your venue and city. Many regions also require certification for staff or volunteers to serve alcohol.

Have water available for free and encourage people to bring their reusable water bottles/containers. Restricting access to water can jeopardize the health of people attending the event. Depending on the venue, this may be more difficult due to the infrastructure of the facility.

Serving

Single-use plastic plates and utensils go straight to the landfill. Is it possible to have food options that do not require utensils? Can you avoid using single-use items? Can you serve food on compostable plates?

Encourage participants to bring reusable cups and water bottles.

Have some straws available for participants who may require them to eat or drink.

Ensure that food is clearly labeled (vegan, gluten-free, kosher, halal, etc) and mark common allergens.

Have a recycling and compost bin in addition to a trashcan to reduce the environmental impact from the event. Make sure these are well marked.

PART IV: CYBER/VIRTUAL EVENTS AND DISSEMINATION

Are you organizing a virtual event? These events can allow people from around the world to connect synchronistically or a-synchronistically (people can watch or listen after the recording). Maybe you will hold a teach-in that you live-stream. Perhaps a concert will happen from living rooms across the planet. This section brings together information about cyber events and the dissemination of materials as there is overlap between them, especially regarding issues of accessibility and sustainability. This section is also useful for organizers of in-person events who wish to broadcast or document their event.

While digital tools expand accessibility in some senses, it is important to note that marginalized communities are more likely to face online harassment including trolling and doxxing. Additionally, if the nature of your event is particularly political, you will want to consider the cybersecurity of your event. Online spaces can be violent spaces.

Online or In-Person + Online

There are numerous types of software that enable online events. This section will mention various providers of software that are controlled by corporations. It can be a challenge to use tools, especially free tools, which are not run by companies that challenge your ethics or sense of justice. Many of these companies will sell your data and/ or engage in unethical practices. It might not be feasible to choose to not use the software from various corporations because oftentimes your audience is already on that social media platform or comfortable with that application. I have provided various resources and you can decide what works for you. To be clear, I am not endorsing any of the services listed below.

Video streams require stable internet connection, which is unavailable to many people. Audio files require less data to download and/or a less stable internet connection. The lower bandwidth option will be more accessible to more folks!

Video Chat Services

Video chat services can be useful for events like book readings, lectures, and panels in which you want the audience to be able to speak and ask questions. Some software allows you to record the video chat and share the footage after the event.

A popular format for online events (at least in 2020) is the video chat service, Zoom. You can use the service for free up to a specified number of users, after which you have to buy a Zoom license. If you are sharing a live musical performance via Zoom, use the strongest wifi available, leave the "automatically adjust microphone volume" box unchecked so that the software doesn't attempt to auto-adjust sound levels based on the preset for speaking voices, and make sure everyone else is on mute. Encourage participants to lower their bandwidth or data usage by turning off their HD video and for people to only share their screens for as long as necessary.

Criticism has been made of Zoom's security and privacy. Security breaches have resulted in "zoombombings"— a phenomenon in which people use the platform to harass the presenter or participants. While Zoom is a popular option, it is not the only one.

Jitsi is a free and open source video conferencing tool (jitsi.org/). Bluejeans is another option. Google Meetings enables auto-captioning. The CoronaVirus Tech Handbook (coronavirustechhandbook.com/ home) is a free resource that offers alternative options to online meetings.

No solution is perfect. Software is ever-changing. It is important to consider cost, encryption, security, simplicity of the user interface, number of users allowed, and the ability to record.

To increase accessibility, providing transcriptions of the audio can make events inclusive of people who are hard or hearing or deaf. Services like otter.ai can assist in this work.

Live Streaming

You can choose to livestream an event that is happening in-person with many people physically present or you can livestream a single speaker or a group call.

Popular live stream platforms include: YouTube (owned in 2020 by Google), Facebook Live, Instagram Stories (owned by Facebook), and Periscope (owned by Twitter). The benefit with these platforms is that all you need is a smartphone (or computer) and a free account. Most of these platforms also include a space where audiences can ask questions or post comments in real time. Platforms like YouTube also make it easy to save the video so that it is available after the event ends so that people can watch the event at a later time, making the event even more accessible. YouTube also auto-generates closed captioning for videos. These captions are imperfect, but are useful for people who are hard of hearing, deaf, or are participating in a second language.

Dissemination After the Event

With the consent of performers, it is possible to record video or audio at your event. The sound quality will be improved if the speaker has a microphone.

Online Video

Services such as YouTube or Vimeo allow you to upload videos from events. You can create a channel to gather videos from related events. Remember to enable auto-generated closed captioning!

Podcast and Other Audio Formats

If you record audio from an event, you can release it as a podcast. Free, open source editing software such as Audacity (https://www.audacityteam.org/download/) can enable you to edit your audio. You would release your podcast after generating a RSS feed and distribute it across podcast players, which aggregate RSS feeds.

You may choose to release audio on music sharing platforms such as Bandcamp. You can create a free account for a limited number of files.

In order to increase accessibility, provide transcripts of the audio.

Website

You may wish to create a website in order to embed videos and audio from the event, share photos, or disseminate other materials from the event. Websites can also be useful for publicity. Website design can impact accessibility, particularly the ability for people who use screen readers. The WCAG (Web Content Accessibility Guidelines) is the main international standard for web accessibility. Things to consider include: font color contrast, font size, not embedding essential information in graphic formats as assistive technologies such as screen readers may not be able to process the text, written description of images, and keyboard navigation. See w3.org/WAI/standards-guidelines/ for more information.

PART V: PUBLICITY

In order for people to participate in your event, they need to know it exists. Your choices surrounding publicity will impact the inclusivity of your event.

Make sure that your publicity includes important details such as time, place, cost, information about accessibility, and how to contact the event organizer about additional accommodations.

Accommodations

Inclusive event organization from a design justice perspective means that the goal is that the event will not require adaptation or modification to remove barriers to participate. However, you still may need to make some accommodations.

On your publicity materials, it will be important to communicate the ways that your event is accessible. However, there may be factors that you did not anticipate. I encourage you to include language on your flyers, website, or other forms of publicity that state something along the lines of:

"We aim to make this an inclusive event. The venue can be reached by public transit (mention the lines/bus routes). It is wheelchair and scooter accessible. On the map below you can find the entrance with a ramp (if different than the main entrance). We are providing whisper translation to French. This is a scent free environment with an all gender bathroom. Childcare will be available if requested 72 hours in advance. Please inform us in advance if you need the following accommodations in order to participate so that we may prepare: assistive listening device, captioning, large print, advance copy of slides, lactation room, or other __. We will be recording the event/live streaming the event for dissemination after."

You may need or want to adjust this note based on the particular circumstances of your event.

Due to scent sensitivities, which can cause nausea and headaches, you can include language on publicity materials such as, "We encourage everyone to help maintain a scent-free environment at the event. Please refrain from wearing perfumes, scented soaps, or scented lotions."

Physical Publicity and Radio

Posters are a classic option. Black ink posters are the cheapest option. I continue to be a fan of cork bulletin boards and flyers taped to street lights as a method of distributing information. This publicity style can lead to chance encounters and help people learn about events that they never would have known about otherwise.

Be mindful of the amount of paper that you use. However, it is important to also note that while we consider cyber space to be intangible, the production and disposal of our computers, phones, and devices have deleterious effects on the environment, as well. Pollution from the metals used to produce our computers renders waterways and landscapes toxic.

Using a large san serif font with a high contrast level to the background is useful for people with dyslexia and people with reduced vision.

Other forms of physical publicity include direct mail and advertisements in newspapers and magazines. You can also consider announcing the event on the radio!

Online Publicity

Publicizing your event online exclusively may limit who will attend the event as not everyone has access to the internet.

Social media platforms are popular choices that can allow you to create an online event announcement and registration list. Many of these platforms use opaque and ever-changing algorithms that impact who sees your event and you often cannot control your listserv. Posting information across platforms increases visibility.

If you want to continue to create subsequent events, consider generating an email listserv in which people can receive news about future shows.

PART VI: AT THE EVENT

Land Acknowledgements

Acknowledging the history of unceded territories on which your event is taking place, as well as the history of the space is an important practice. Land or territory acknowledgements occur at the beginning of public events. They are often concise and follow a format of: "I want to acknowledge that we are on the traditional territory of [nation names]," though they can be more comprehensive. It is important that if you are giving the acknowledgement, you know how to properly pronounce the name of the nation or community. It is even better if you can learn the name of the nation or community in its original language. Ideally a member of that community will give the opening address. You need to financially compensate this person and provide an honorarium gift.

The violence of the colonization of North America is not relegated to the past. The ongoing impacts of colonization shape our present society. Land acknowledgements raise awareness about Indigenous presence and land rights. They encourage settlers to recognize the history and political reality of the United States and Canada, which is often omitted from school curriculum.

Native Land Digital (native-land.ca) has created an invaluable resource, including a map that indicates Indigenous territories, languages, and treaties, a teacher's guide, and a list of further resources to help people understand the histories of the lands that we live and work on.

There is some critique that land acknowledgements are token gestures, especially when the people doing them and the audience hearing them do not think about the steps beyond acknowledging the territory where the event is taking place. How can we have reconciliation if we don't have justice? In response, Chelsea Vowel, a Métis writer and scholar from the Plains Cree speaking community of Lac Ste. Anne, Alberta, writes: "If we think of territorial acknowledgments as sites of potential disruption, they can be transformative acts that to some extent undo Indigenous erasure. I believe this is true as long as these acknowledgments discomfit both those speaking and hearing the words. The fact of Indigenous presence should force non-Indigenous peoples to confront their own place on these lands." – Chelsea

Vowel, Métis, Beyond Territorial Acknowledgements (apihtawikosisan. com/2016/09/beyond-territorial-acknowledgments/).

Land Acknowledgements are merely a starting place. They do not replace the necessary work of reconciliation. The Truth and Reconciliation Commission of Canada's 94 calls to action (trc.ca/assets/pdf/Calls_to_Action_English2. pdf) provide a framework for this work.

Acknowledging Other Forms of Violence Related to the Space of the Event

The United States and Canada built their nations through the practice of enslaving African and Indigenous peoples. The violent legacy of slavery continues across society ranging from racialized economic disparity, high rates of incarceration of people of color, and lower life expectancies and less access to medical care for communities of color.

I hold many events at McGill University. The founder of McGill University, James McGill, was a slave-owner and he economically benefited through his choice to enslave others. With this money, McGill University came into existence. I acknowledge this fact at the start of events I host on campus as the histories of violence within our institutions continue to influence and impact the kinds of conversations that are had.

I encourage you to think critically about the role of space in the events that we organize.

Question and Answer Periods

After lectures, teach-ins, artist talks, book readings, and panels, question and answer periods are common practice. During these Q&A periods, there is a tendency for people with more privilege to raise their hands first and dominate the microphone. It can be useful to remind people to be aware of the space that they are occupying in the room. If as an organizer you are the one choosing who is asking questions, think about the demographics of the people who are asking most of the questions.

By providing a short pause of 2 minutes between the performance/talk and the Q&A period, people will have time to gather their thoughts and reflect upon their questions before asking them. As the organizer you also can begin the question period with one of your own in order to ease the audience into the Q&A period.

If you have a microphone, please either ask audience members to ask their questions into the microphone or pass a microphone to the question speaker in order that people who are hard of hearing can hear. If there is no microphone for audience questions, please ask that the person answering the question repeat the question before answering it.

If you are worried about encountering the dreaded "more of a comment than a question," no questions from shy audience members, or the possibility of trolling and/or harassment at the event, it is possible to collect audience questions in advance or pass a hat to collect questions. This way you can filter some of the questions. If your event is happening in a digital space, it is possible to filter questions similarly by asking people to send their questions in advance or through an online platform.

A Q&A period can be wonderful for audience members to connect with the speaker. However, it is important to set a time frame. Many of us have encountered a Q&A period that seems to go on and on and on. This can be hard on an audience and on the speaker. Check in advance with your speaker if perhaps questions can continue in a more informal way after the event. If there is a merchandise "merch" table with the speaker's art, music, or books, audience questions will likely continue there.

DAY OF THE EVENT TIPS AND TRICKS

• Always have tape, paper, and a bold marker on you— no matter the kind of event. Ideally you can have masking tape and duct tape. You never know if you will need to make a sign with arrows to direct people where to go. Masking tape won't rip paint off of walls. Duct tape has a wide variety of applications. Markers, pens, and paper are useful if— shocker— you need to write anything down.

• You will want to have clear and visible signs for accessible entrances, parking, washrooms, public phones, transit points, and other conveniences.

• Arrive early! If you are the organizer, ideally you are the first to arrive. I like to have time to center myself mentally in the venue and prepare whatever materials are necessary. I don't want performers, speakers, or attendees to show up before me and feel lost.

• Bring chargers, cords, USB sticks, connector cables, and a laptop if you have one! I live in Canada and just from walking to a venue, the winter cold can kill my phone battery. Oftentimes, presenters and performers and I plan to contact one another by texting before an event. To have a dead phone battery can increase stress unnecessarily. Having backup computer chargers, batteries, extension cords, and USB sticks can be game changers. I often hold events in rooms where I haven't been able to try the tech before. I bring my own computer, connector cables (such as USB to VGA or USB to HDMI), and USB sticks in case the presenter's computer doesn't work with the tech set up of the venue.

• Do a soundcheck and check all necessary technology. If a video is embedded in a Powerpoint or similar presentation, check that it works. There is still always a risk that the tech will still fail. Have you made a backup plan?

• Check pronunciation. Before the event, always check how people pronounce their names and their preferred pronouns before introducing them to the stage. Even if someone's name seems obvious, I still double check pronunciation. Practice the pronunciation of the nations mentioned in your land acknowledgement. Make sure you have the right acronyms and organization names, especially of your sponsors or co-collaborators.

• After the event, I always follow up with the performer to thank them for their work. If there is any last minute paperwork that we have to process, I try to make sure that we can do that soon after the event when details are fresh in everyone's mind. If you need signatures from people, you'll make sure you get those before any travelling happens!

THANK YOU

Dear readers, after reading this handbook, I hope you are inspired to organize inclusive events! I hope you can benefit from the process of my learning from my mistakes.

This handbook would not be possible without the body of feminist and social justice literature that continues to shape me and my work. Thank you to the writers, thinkers, activists, and artists who inspire and challenge me. Thank you to the activists in the disability rights movement who continually bring awareness to the importance of accessibility. Thank you to everyone who has ever attended or supported an event that I have organized. Thank you for your patience as I learned what worked or didn't work. Thank you to every group and individual with whom I have had the pleasure to collaborate. Thank you to Amy Edward and Margeaux Reed for your edits.

MORE RESOURCES

For further reading, check out these free resources:

Design Justice: Community-Led Practices to Build the Worlds We Need by Sasha Costanza-Chock (MIT Press, 2020) is available open access at: mitpress.mit.edu/books/design-justice

Nicole J. Georges' podcast "Sagittarian Matters" episode from May 20, 2016 in which she interviews music manager Tara Perkins has a great discussion around the politics of paying artists.

The Accessible Campus Checklist for Planning Accessible Conferences has some useful tips:

accessiblecampus.ca/wp-content/uploads/2016/12/A-Checklist-for-Planning-Accessible-Events-1.pdf

Native Land Digital's maps and resources: native-land.ca

For more on auto-captioning tools and delivering accessible presentations, see the work of Rua M. Williams: ruamae.com/disability-advocacy/delivering-accessible-presentations/.

ABOUT THE AUTHOR

Alex Ketchum has organized hundreds of events, including lectures, battle of the bands, book readings, organic pumpkin festivals, workshops, and art shows. She is a professor of Gender, Sexuality, Feminist, and Social Studies at McGill University. Her PhD dissertation was about the history of feminist restaurants, cafes, and coffeehouses in the United States and Canada from 1972-1989. Based on this research, Dr. Ketchum published the zine "How to Start a Feminist Restaurant" (Microcosm, 2018) and created thefeministrestaurantproject.com. She is the founder and organizer of the SSHRC (Social Science and Humanities Research Council of Canada) funded, Feminist and Accessible Publishing, Communications, Technologies Speaker and Workshop Series (feministandaccessiblepublishingandtechnology.com). Her PhD and MA in History and Women and Gender Studies are from McGill University and her Honors BA in Feminist, Gender, and Sexuality Studies is from Wesleyan University. Her work integrates food, environmental, technological, and gender history. Alex Ketchum is committed to accessible publishing practices and public scholarship. For more information, visit alexketchum.ca.